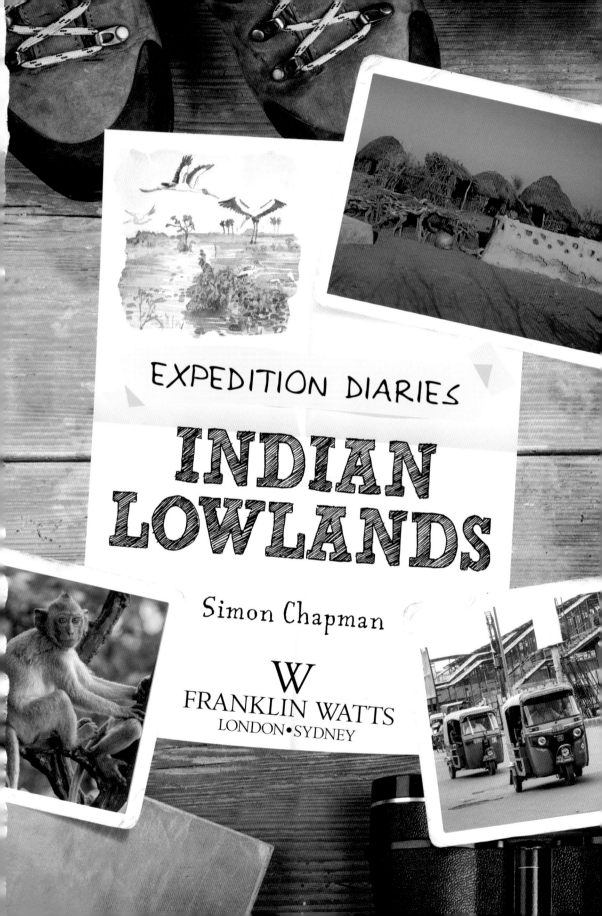

EXPEDITION DIARIES

INDIAN LOWLANDS

Simon Chapman

W
FRANKLIN WATTS
LONDON·SYDNEY

Expedition to India

The plan is to look for tigers and monkeys in northern India, which forms part of the Indo-Gangetic Plain. It's still monsoon season, so I'm expecting some trouble with the weather, and I'll need to plan the trip carefully. I'll be heading into a variety of different habitats, including floodplains, desert and mountain foothills – so I really need to be ready for anything!

Kit list
– Lightweight easy-to-dry shirt and trousers – sand/khaki coloured

The rhesus macaque monkeys I will be studying have been 'habituated' to (used to seeing) people in dull-coloured clothes. Wearing khaki will allow me to get closer to see what they are doing.

– Trainers

– Lightweight boots with good grip

– Sandals for canoeing

– Fleece jumper for the cooler nights

– Sunhat, sun block, water bottle

To buy in New Delhi
I'm not bringing a raincoat, despite the high chance of monsoon rains (which will soak through anything!) – but I will buy an umbrella in New Delhi. No need for camping gear, as I'm mostly staying in lodges, so I'm packing really light and taking just a small daypack.

INDO-GANGETIC PLAIN

The Indo-Gangetic Plain includes the deltas of the Brahmaputra river, Ganges river and the Indus river valley. The three main rivers deposit fertile soil across the plain - perfect for growing rice, wheat and other crops. In the east, the plain experiences light rains or drought in winter, but heavy rainfall in the summer, creating swamps and lakes. The west is drier and includes the Thar Desert (left of map). The open grasslands of the plain are home to Indian elephants, rhinoceros and striped hyenas. In woodland areas Bengal tigers hunt for prey. Water-buffalo and the mugger crocodile can be found in the wetter regions.

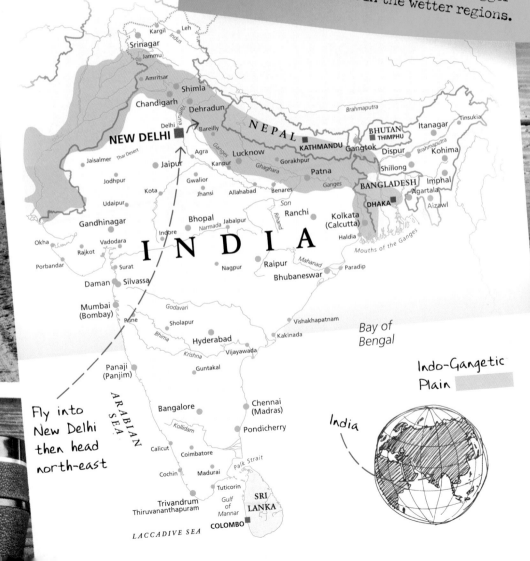

Fly into New Delhi then head north-east

Indo-Gangetic Plain

India

TRAVEL PRECAUTIONS

I'll be travelling alone for most of the time, so I'll need to take precautions to make sure my valuables are protected.

Security
- Money belt to wear under my trousers, containing my passport, credit cards and most of my money.
- Scans: pictures of my passport, flight details and important addresses in case the originals are lost. I'll keep printed-out copies in my rucksack and in various pockets. I'll also email myself the picture files so I can get the information online if I need to.

Injections
I've got to have a rabies injection for this trip. I'm scared of savage dogs ... and of getting bitten by an infected monkey!

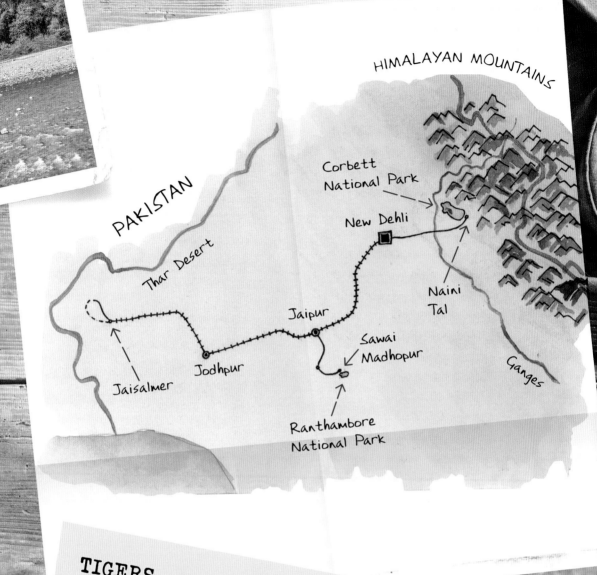

HIMALAYAN MOUNTAINS

PAKISTAN

Thar Desert

Corbett
National Park

New Dehli

Naini
Tal

Jaipur

Sawai
Madhopur

Jaisalmer

Jodhpur

Ganges

Ranthambore
National Park

TIGERS

There are only an estimated 3,900 wild tigers in the world and 2,500 of those are Bengal tigers living in India, Bangladesh, Nepal and Bhutan. Bengal tigers are apex predators, which means no animals eat them. But Bengal tigers are threatened by habitat loss. Farmland now surrounds many of the jungle areas where they live. Small populations of tigers become isolated and in-breeding leads to unhealthy young.

New Delhi

**Mrs Culaco's Guesthouse,
New Delhi, 19 AUG, 6.30 PM**

So many experiences since I've arrived.
Early afternoon seemed like late evening
as the sky got steadily darker until a
storm broke out. **One of the lightning
blasts sounded just like a** huge **explosiOn!**

The way into Delhi was flat and very, very green. There were stacks of birds swooping over the road and water buffalo in the marshy bits by the roadside (left). There were cows grazing on the grass central reservation!

As the bus rolled into town the streets became lined with rickety shop fronts, tangles of overhead wiring, auto rickshaws and (more) cows wandering about.

The auto rickshaws swarmed everywhere, racing around like mosquitoes.

The crows in Delhi are really tough birds.

They're everywhere and look like something out of a horror film. I saw two crows pecking a rat to death – that's how tough the crows are here! Can't wait to get my gear together and head out of the city.

FINALLY ...

After wading through water-logged streets and dodging mad traffic, I turned into a side street with quaint wooden houses, gardens full of flowers and twittering birds. A little island of calm!

7

Monsooned!

I've been monsooned on!

This is different from being rained on.
Sitting in the porch of the hotel in dry
clothes watching the rain come down in sheets.

Morning

Went into central Delhi
to get some supplies in
an auto rickshaw.

The roads in places must have
been nearly 30 cm deep in water,
with little kids swimming around
in the pools.

In the bazaars there are narrow
alleys with people living and selling
things from what look like narrow
sheds. My arms are constantly
being tugged by small, bright-eyed
children begging for money.

The light is a really eerie yellow and there are stacks of black kites (Milvus migrans) swooping around and sitting on the lampposts.

Getting out of New Delhi tomorrow. Taxi booked to

Corbett National Park,

which is in the Himalayan foothills, 160 km or so north of Delhi. Jim Corbett (left), who the reserve is named after, was an English tiger hunter in the 1930s who decided he would rather conserve tigers than kill them.

9

Car Crash

21 AUG, morning

Heading north out of Delhi, although the driver doesn't seem to know his way out of the city. He keeps stopping to ask for directions.

21 AUG, mid-afternoon

Roughly six hours into the journey after:

- lots of traffic jams
- overtaking into oncoming traffic
- buffalo, dogs and sometimes monkeys in the road
- cycle rickshaws insanely overloaded with piles of sugar cane
- one elephant (that was on an overpass in the middle of Delhi)

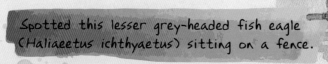

Spotted this lesser grey-headed fish eagle (*Haliaeetus ichthyaetus*) sitting on a fence.

I'm near Kashipur by the roadside after the taxi driver crashed into a tractor. I'm a bit shaken up, but apart from some neck pain I don't seem to have suffered any serious injuries.

The same fish eagle lunging for a fish.

The driver seems fine, too, which is more than can be said for his taxi. He tried to get through the gap between the tractor and the edge of the road. He finally slammed on the brakes when he realised the tractor driver wasn't going to move. Too late. Now the taxi has a v-shaped bonnet, and a crowd has sprung out of nowhere (it is just fields all around) as both drivers have a massive argument.

View out across the flooded fields.

LATER ...

Faced with the problem of how to get to Corbett National Park, I got on a bus and now I'm sitting on a wet seat. (It's not raining, but a toddler who was sitting here before me left it wet with wee – urgh!). I eventually got to Ramnagar and took a taxi to the park.

Dawn Ride

22 AUG, dawn

I'm writing this on the back of an elephant as we head through the grasslands floodplain. I'm having trouble concentrating though.

I've been awake since 2.00 AM, being sick

in the lodge where I'm staying.

I think the food I bought from a street vendor was dodgy. And I haven't taken enough care purifying my drinking water.

No tigers yet - I think I heard one, though. The roar sounded more like **'hroompf!'**

It's freezing cold. I'm watching spotted deer (above) and wild boar, with scenic dawn views across forested Himalayan foothills.

The forests are mainly made up of tall, straight sal trees (*Shorea robusta*) with a little low undergrowth (below). There are other gnarled-looking trees and 'strangler' figs where the forest opens out.

Fig tree near the camp.

In the park, the floodplain habitat of the river is called *chaur*, and was once agricultural land.

FLOODPLAINS

A floodplain is the flat ground surrounding a river before it meets higher ground. This area is flooded when rains are heavy. Floodwaters deposit fertile soil along the floodplain, making it a good place for growing crops during the rest of the year.

LATER ...

I've been sick over the side of the elephant. Saw some gharials (*Gavialis gangeticus*), though (below). They were in a lovely blue pool at the foot of a rapid in the Ramganga river. The river looks excellent for canoeing!

13

Tiger Trail

Morning view of the Himalayas - about an hour's jeep drive uphill from the national park. I'm travelling with Mr Puri, who is a park guide and Dani Ram, his assistant.

There are tracks of tigers (a big one) and elephants. Mr Puri says that the wild elephants wander really high into the mountains.

The temperature is
so cold
up here that I am wearing most of my clothes!

Grey langur sitting on a rock.

The jungle is low and thorny. There's not a big variety of animals; just lots of wild buffalo and big groups of grey langurs.

We drove down narrow paths, ducking as we scraped past thorny branches. We saw lots of grey langurs, spotted deer and the back end of an elephant (and lots of elephant dung!) The jungle was really atmospheric, especially sitting at the swampy lake with its hundreds of storks, ducks and black-winged stilts (right), also buffalo, crocodiles, and some jackals that were quite near to where I was sitting.

LATER ...

Actually, some of the crocodiles were too close when I went for a swim in a rocky river later. It was only when I put my glasses on afterwards that I realised they were there!

Lakeside Trek

A giant squirrel was nibbling leaves outside my bedroom window early this morning. As I lay in bed, all I could hear was a strange munching sound. There was also a land monitor lizard nearby.

I'm on a lakeside walk with Dani Ram. I waded out to an island in knee deep water. Unfortunately all the white-necked storks on it flew away when I got there.

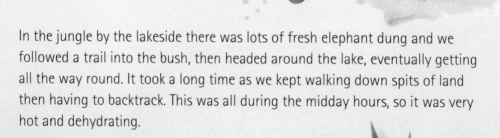

In the jungle by the lakeside there was lots of fresh elephant dung and we followed a trail into the bush, then headed around the lake, eventually getting all the way round. It took a long time as we kept walking down spits of land then having to backtrack. This was all during the midday hours, so it was very hot and dehydrating.

I've just returned from a sunset walk by the lake.

We swam the channel to get to the bit where I found elephant dung yesterday, then walked a lot further and

spotted a wild elephant

... OK, it was a long way in the distance.

It must've been quite big though, because what we thought were

pigs next to it turned out to be buffalo!

When it headed into the jungle we started back.

LAKE HABITAT

As a freshwater biome, lakes provide a constant supply of water to the living things that inhabit the lake, such as fish, and those that visit the area to feed, such as crocodiles. This is especially important during the dry season when freshwater is hard to come by. Trees and reeds grow in the damp soil at the water's edge, while plants, such as water lilies, grow in the lake itself.

Found this tree frog sitting in my toilet!

17

Monkey Business

I have just been followed home by a baby mouse deer. The adults are cute, but the babies are just the **cutest things ever.**

The mother bolted off, leaving its fawn behind, which kept following us. Eventually, Dani Ram walked several times around a telegraph pole with it following until it got confused. We hope its mother collected it after we left.

NIGHT-TIME NOTE

I'm terrified that the ceiling fan in my bedroom at the lodge is going to wiggle itself off and slice me in half while I sleep. The end has worked itself off and vibrates from side to side.

18

I woke up this morning to see young macaques frolicking around in the bushes by the window.

While we wait for more news on tiger activity, I'm helping out on a monkey 'follow' over the next few days. The macaques are quite used to having people around, provided you wear camouflage clothing and stay quiet. My job will be to follow a group of them, draw where they go on a map and write down what they are doing.

This mongoose just peeped its head around the corner of the building!

LATER ...

Lots of grey langurs around the hut. They bound along in a springy, bum-up sort of way. Though the langurs are much bigger than the macaques, it is the macaques that pick on them. The langurs also groom the macaques from time to time.

19

Macaque Follow

Following monkeys is not as easy as I had thought! For a start there's a lot of crawling through undergrowth, then you lose them.

Female – redder face

Bluish buttocks

Golden fur on back and on thighs →

Lighter underneath – greyish fur

I thought I had lost the troupe in the bushes,

so I sat down under a tree where a young male was resting, reckoning where there's one, there must be many. Pretty soon I was proved right, as I was surrounded by monkeys! Now they are everywhere, grooming each other (picking off ticks and parasites) while some youngsters mess around in the bushes.

I feel like I'm in a wildlife TV programme!

RHESUS MACAQUE (MACACA MULATTA)

Rhesus macaques are found in Afghanistan, Pakistan, India, southeast Asia and China. They are primates with pale brown fur and pink faces. They live in noisy troupes of up to 200 animals and eat roots, fruits, seeds and insects. These monkeys adapt to many different types of habitat and may be found in grasslands, forests and mountainous areas.

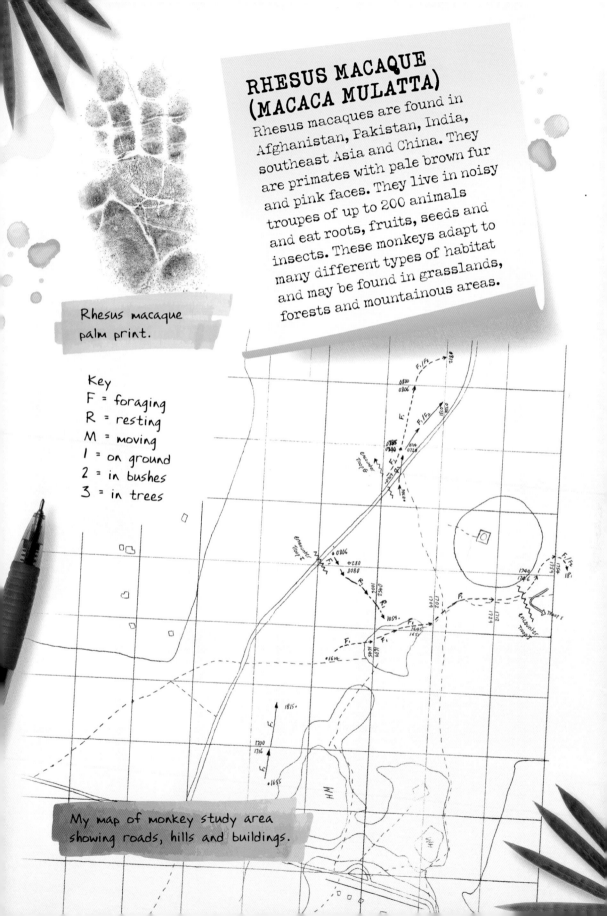

Rhesus macaque palm print.

Key
F = foraging
R = resting
M = moving
1 = on ground
2 = in bushes
3 = in trees

My map of monkey study area showing roads, hills and buildings.

Lost in the Forest

This afternoon I followed a troupe of macaque monkeys as they moved through the forest. Now it's nearly sunset, the monkeys are beginning to bed down for the night, and I have just realised that it's really late.

I have to get back!

I'm sitting in the
oncoming darkness,

hooting like the monkeys do (as this is what Dani Ram told me to do if we get separated). But no one is answering, except for some animal making a cough-barking sound (could be muntjac deer ... or leopard?) which sent some grey langurs bounding off a nearby fallen tree. I'm not panicking yet though, and will head west until I find the road.

LATER ...

At least my position estimate was right. I wandered back, blowing my whistle until I heard the jeep driving along the road. The driver had been pretty worried – he thought I might have been bitten by a snake.

INDIAN COBRA (NAJA NAJA)

I didn't see this cobra in the forest, but it is exactly the kind of snake that the driver was worried about. (I paid a monkey-owning snake charmer about 60p to sketch this but I had to finish it later as it tried to lunge at me. Luckily he held it back.)

29 AUG

We cycled around some ruins this afternoon and then got blown by the wind back to the rest house, along the dam road by the edge of the lake.

This chestnut headed bee-eater (*Merops leschenaulti*) was in a dogfight with a large flying beetle. The bird made several acrobatic swoops, but still didn't catch it.

This white statue stands out against the grey rock.

Cave Statues

There is mushy and sandy earth inside the cave, sloping upwards. Somebody has cut a slot out near the entrance. I read that Buddhist artefacts were found in some of these caves and people came up to loot them.

Bas-relief of a demon in a temple near the cave.

CAVE-DWELLERS
Animals that live in caves adapt to the darkness of their habitat by using their highly-developed senses of hearing, touch and smell. Bats, such as the bent-winged bat, live in the many temples, caves and ruins found throughout India. Bat and bird droppings often line the cave floor, providing food for bacteria, fungi and insects.

24

There were many statues carved into the rock face by hand, but the 8-m high Buddha (below) was the largest. This was still a local pilgrimage site, with people walking along a path and chanting.

Grey langurs on the path back from the cave.

I sketched this youngster, whose legs appeared very spindly.

The rest of the troupe are feeding in low trees. The langurs are quite chilled and don't seem overly bothered by people here.

Still No Tigers

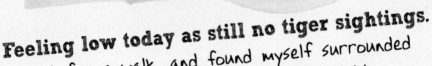

**30 AUG, late afternoon
walk on a wasteland area**

Feeling low today as still no tiger sightings.

I went for a walk, and found myself surrounded by discarded plastic bottles and other litter.

A line of bushes ran along the edge of stagnant pools and creeks whose edges have been eroded by cows' hoofs.

I could see over a hundred cows in the distance

across the marshy grassland between the road and the lake.

There are lots of birds here:

black-winged stilts, egrets, larks, even a stork-billed kingfisher (right), as well as two different types of parakeet.

Suddenly four jackals appeared on the lakeside.

They caused quite a stir, with birds flying off, and didn't seem that interested in hunting. Two of the dogs (below) seem much younger, and could be cubs from this year.

Just before sunset I spotted a young black kite on top of a fence post, eating a white-feathered bird. There were crows arguing beneath.

LATER ...

Sitting on a bare rocky mound, locally called Crocodile Rock, with parakeets and doves flying all around.

TOURIST POLLUTION

Many tourists visit this area to experience the beautiful landscape and fascinating wildlife. They bring much needed money to the local economy. But, the presence of tourists can often threaten the very existence of the plants and animals these people have come to see.

Guide Hire

While I was having breakfast, a mongoose walked past the rest house where I'm staying. I wonder if it's the same one as before?

I've decided to hire a guide to improve my chances of seeing a tiger. Guyan owns a jeep (which he's very proud of) and knows many of the places where they are seen regularly.

There are huge herds of buffalo here, and dozens of waterholes

(though I am not sure that the buffalo are truly wild).

Many of the waterholes have crocodiles, sometimes half-submerged, sometimes on the shore with their mouths gaping to cool themselves down. Guyan tells me that the larger ones attack the buffalo.

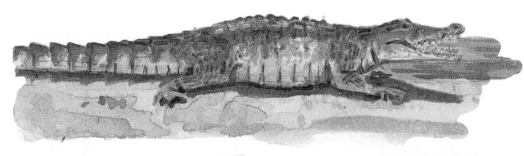

CROCODILES
There are three main types of crocodile found in India: the mugger, gharial and estuarine. The mugger crocodile is considered to be a vulnerable species, but the gharial is critically endangered, with only 235 believed to live in the wild.

Afternoon

Still no tigers, but there's so much wildlife all around.

After driving back across open plains, at a muddy pool I was struck by all the different types of bird so close together.

LATER ...
Saw these little green bee-eaters at sunset when we were driving back. Green clouds of them rose up from the sandy track.

Spotted a Leopard!

1 SEP, 6.10 PM, driving back to the rest house

Now I'm driving alongside a wetland swamp covered with lily pads. Masses of painted storks are nesting noisily in the bushes.

I spotted a night heron,
a painted stork and white ibis
and I can even see an

elephant in the distance.

This monitor lizard waddling along in a weird zig-zag motion.

Just spotted a leopard.
(No pun intended.)

The jeep just rounded a bend and this leopard was lying on the sand by the side of the track. In all of three seconds it had woken up and bounded into the bushes.

LEOPARDS

The Indian leopard is found in tropical, temperate, deciduous and alpine forests across India; it is also found in grassland areas. Leopards hunt by night for prey such as wild dogs, hog deer and wild boar. Leopards often bring their prey up into the trees to keep their food away from other large cats, such as tigers, who share their territory.

The driver checked his phone and said we had to leave the reserve by 6.30 pm when the gate would be closed.

6.40 PM

The sun is setting – it's a reddish-peach colour – and to the right is an oblong chunk of storm cloud that keeps flashing from the inside with lightning. Occasional ripples of light pulse through the cloud.

Leaving Corbett

I've decided that this will be my last day in Corbett National Park. I'm going to move west to another region where tigers can also be seen in the wild.

We took the jeep out this morning to look at elephants. The sun is rising and the grass around the lake is covered with mist.

Late morning

Driving round out of the forest as it opened up, there is a lone bull (male) elephant standing right on the edge of the road.

Now the bull elephant is getting closer and closer to the jeep, so we have to move on.

There is a young elephant – about 6 m to our right – with its mother just behind in the bushes. The driver said not to knock on the roof of the jeep – which is what I must have been doing as I sketch.

LATER ...

Watched a small herd of elephants walking alongside the water. I've seen them splashing around before, but not now. Perhaps they can sense there are crocodiles around.

Back in Dehli

3 SEP, back to Delhi

I caught a bus back to Delhi. I'm sitting next to an elderly woman, who keeps pointing out sights to see.

Whenever I doze off she prods me. When her husband falls asleep, she grabs him by the ear and pulls until he comes to his senses.

She and her husband looked through my glasses and looked through this diary. Her daughter, who is sitting behind, is playing tricks, such as tying her plaits to the seat or swiping her headscarf.

Afternoon – Delhi

I ended up at a railway office reserving tickets to head west to the hot, dry state of Rajasthan. Went for a stroll through the bazaar at Paharganj (above).

Indian Pioneer butterfly in Lodhi Gardens.

As I'm getting a night train out of New Delhi, I've spent most of the day hanging out in Lodhi Gardens. There are old tombs here with domes that look like mini versions of the Taj Mahal, and trees with birds flitting between them -

it's nice to get away from the city traffic!

On the way back I found a café and had some excellent samosas and masala dosa (pancakes rolled around veggy curry).

MIGRATORY HABITS

Delhi is a safe haven to more than 250 species of migratory birds, 150 species of butterflies and 10 species each of animals comprising hyena, fox, jackal, nilgai, mongoose and porcupines etc. Wildlife experts fear climate change and a break in the food chain due to rising levels of pollution, will force these animals to migrate to other parts of the world.

LATER ...

Met up with a guy called Justin, who is headed to Jaisalmer to trek through the Thar Desert.

35

Jaisalmer, Rajasthan

I'm heading west with Justin to join his camel trek. He thinks it will take about three days. I've got nearly two weeks left in India, so I should still get to Ranthambore National Park.

Jaisalmer

The countryside outside the window varies from flat scrub with some sand dunes, to greener areas where maize and other crops grow. Small, light-green trees dot the landscape. Occasionally you see people, stray dogs and camels.

At one point earlier there was a mass of really large vultures.

We are sitting on yellow wooden plank benches, and just above my head is another bench on which somebody is sleeping. There are lots of compartments like this on the train. Not comfortable.

Justin is really ill today.

He is lying on the bed in his room with a roaring temperature and absolutely no energy.

We're supposed to be heading into the desert tomorrow,

so I don't know what is going to happen. It's his high temperature that worries me most. I have to make sure he doesn't get dehydrated, and have given him some anti-sickness tablets I had.

The old town of Jaisalmer is inside high-turreted, yellow sandstone walls, and is like something out of *The Arabian Nights*. There are temples to the elephant-headed Hindu god, Ganesh, and most of the buildings are covered with intricately carved patterns (above). In amongst all these narrow streets, goats and cows roam freely.

LATER ...

Headed out into the desert by jeep. Justin isn't here. He's too sick to travel. He's back in Jaisalmer, and I'm a bit worried about him.

37

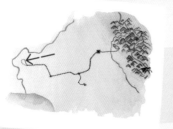

Into the Thar Desert

I actually slept quite well in the open under a damp quilt with the occasional beetle crawling over me.

Having a poo though was quite an experience,

as by the time I had finished, my deposits had been broken into chunks and taken away by dung beetles (they lay their eggs in it).

Near a deserted palace, there's a walled garden and carved outbuildings all decaying slowly in the heat. One of the darker rooms was alive with bats and the buzzing of wasps' nests.

In places the desert scenery of rocks and occasional sand dunes gives way to grasslands, where the bushes are greener after the first rains in several years. It's pleasant in the low, cool morning sun. **There are birds twittering overhead and large low-flying hawks.**

Feeling unwashed, but otherwise not too bad. The camel riding is long and hard.

Lunchtime

We have reached a large oasis: a shallow lake with many trees and lots of wading birds. We wallow in the water to cool off.

Some sort of 'thick knee' or stone curlew with an **oversize shovel beak.**

Black-winged stilts (in pairs) are ridiculously dainty. I even saw a Chinkara gazelle about 40 m away flashing its black-and-white tail as it bounded away.

39

Desert Heat

7 SEP, sunset

Travelling along the course of a tree-lined dried-up river bed,

I saw a peacock. This is where they originate from; Indian scrub jungle. I also saw a jungle fowl – an ancestor of domesticated chickens.

8 SEP Camp 3, midday, rest break

We are camped between a stone water tank and a deserted-looking village. I am spending most of my time boiling water in my mess tins to purify it, as I'm worried because I drank lake water earlier.

Very, very hot as we head back to Jaisalmer.

The scenery has become boring; parched, dark-brown rocky earth with only the odd village to break the monotony.

9 SEP, afternoon, back in Jaisalmer

When I got back I promptly drank down one-and-a-half litres of water. Justin was half asleep in his hotel room when I checked on him. He is still pretty ill and is staying in Jaisalmer.

We say our goodbyes before I head to catch a night train east to Jodhpur ... **and then to Jaipur.**

10 SEP, 9 PM, at Jodhpur station

Another night train tonight and various buses should get me to Ranthambore National Park sometime tomorrow – or the next day. I'm now worried I'm running out of time before my flight home, but Ranthambore is said to be the best place in all of India for spotting a wild tiger.

11 SEP, Jaipur

Jaipur is all hustle and bustle. There are working elephants here, and a lot of monkeys –

mostly langurs.

ONWARDS ...

I can see nilgai (right) as we pass along the road. They are large, and have a sloping back and white ankle bands.

Ranthambore

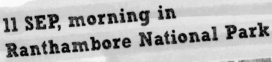

I'm with a guide in his old jeep. We've been driving through the low, dry forest, set amongst scrubby, rocky hills.

We have driven past several lakes with sambhar deer and wild boar wallowing and grazing, as well as lots of wildfowl and storks.

No tigers though ...

A few minutes after I painted this sambhar doe (left), a fawn suckled from her. Sambhars (*Rusa unicolor*) are the biggest type of deer here. The smaller spotted deer, or chital, is more common.

Getting towards sunset

A quick sketch across one of the lakes towards the old Rajput fortress on the ridge. The reddish colour in the foreground is algae in the water.

I can see people climbing stone steps that lead all the way up to a temple. The jeep driver said that sometimes people see tigers along the way - and sometimes they get attacked...

Huge brown fish owl, hunting on the lake.

RANTHAMBORE NATIONAL PARK

The park is a green 'island' of jungle amongst fields. People living at the edges come into the reserve for firewood, reducing the jungle size and putting them in danger. The tigers and leopards (which mainly live at the edges away from the tigers) have less room. There are around 30 tigers inside the reserve.

LATER ...

My arms and most of my body have come out in a mysterious rash. I'm hoping it's just an allergic reaction ...

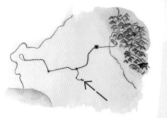

Last Drive

Tomorrow I head back to Jaipur, then to Delhi and my flight back home.

I've jumped in the jeep again, and we've stopped by a small swampy lake after driving on the trails. Not even any tiger tracks this morning.

Indian darter (Anhinga melanogaster) drying wings.

Guess what I've just seen?

A young tigress came up to the edge of the long grass by the lake's edge where we were resting in the jeep. So lucky! She picked up a dead spotted deer. I had a perfect viewing position. She stood right in front of the jeep, long enough for me to sketch her portrait. I think there's another tiger nearby – at least the grass to the right keeps twitching.

The tigress eventually slunk away, dragging her kill backwards. We have driven off up one side of the valley. The forest is drier and stunted, making it less attractive for hunting tigers. There are nilgai and chinkara gazelles around hopefully.

Just after lunch

I can't believe what just happened! An adult male leopard crossed the road in front of the jeep as we were re-entering the national park.

Then it padded into the forest. It wasn't particularly bothered by us, so we got a good long look at it. I've scanned through the photos I took. Even though the leopard was so close you can hardly see it. It is that well camouflaged. Incredible!

What an amazing last day.

13 SEP, back in Delhi

I'm all ready for the flight home. The city feels even busier now, after being out in the forest.

I've just seen a Santa Claus on skis on the back of a cycle rickshaw! **Delhi is a wonderful, crazy place!**

Back Home

On my last day I saw an elephant being led down the edge of the highway that leads into New Delhi city centre. There were tower blocks to either side, and cars speeding alongside beeping their horns. Only in India! This country is such a shock on the senses. I've travelled from teeming cities to jungles where I've seen leopards and monkeys, and I've ridden a camel across a desert! Best of all though was seeing a tiger! I hope that people can continue to protect them and the truly wild places in this magnificent country.

I met up with Justin back in Delhi. His illness got better the day I left Jaisalmer. He carried on with his travels in India to the high Himalayas of Sikkim state, right down to Kerala in the far south. I still see Justin a lot - he married my sister!

CORBETT NATIONAL PARK

Named after the tiger-hunter turned nature-lover and conservationist, Jim Corbett, this park became the first national park of India in 1936. It is famed for its large population of tigers and its stunning landscapes. It covers an area of 1,288 km² and is home to 50 types of mammal, 577 birds, 25 reptiles and a wide variety of trees and grasses. Tourists visit the park in large numbers to see the wildlife.

The park is divided into five different zones, including the hilly terrain of the Durga Devi Zone and the Bijrani Zone, which is the best area to spot the Bengal tiger. The park is responsible for starting a number of conservation projects to protect tigers, crocodiles and elephants.

A Bengal tiger on the prowl.

Glossary

alpine Connected to high mountains.

bazaar A market with lots of small shops and stalls.

biome A type of natural environment, such as a forest or lake.

Buddha Siddhartha Gautama (born in the 6th century BCE), the man who founded the Buddhist religion.

conserve To protect something and stop it being destroyed.

deciduous Type of tree that loses its leaves every year.

dehydrate Lose too much water.

delta The low-lying area where numerous river distributaries meet the sea.

dogfight A mid-air fight, for example between birds.

endangered species A group of animals that are so few in number that they are in danger of dying out.

erode Gradually wear away.

fertile soil Land where crops or plants grow very well.

food chain Living things linked because one eats the other.

foothill A hill close to higher hills or mountains.

grassland A large area of open land covered in grasses.

habitat The normal environment of a living thing.

in-breeding When closely related animals breed with each other, producing young that are often weaker or unhealthy.

migratory Describing animals that move from one area to another with the seasons.

monsoon Several weeks of very heavy rain, falling in the summer in South Asia (and again in the winter in some areas).

national park An area of land (or sea) owned by the government where the wildlife is protected.

oasis An area in a desert where water occurs and plants grow.

predator An animal that kills other animals to eat them.

primate Animals that includes apes, monkeys and humans.

stagnant Still water, which often smells bad.

temperate Area of the world where the climate is mild.

troupe A group of monkeys that live together.

waterhole A place where wild animals gather to drink.

Index

Franklin Watts
First published in Great Britain in 2018 by
The Watts Publishing Group

Copyright © The Watts Publishing Group 2018

All rights reserved

Executive editor: Adrian Cole
Series designer: Elaine Wilkinson
Design manager: Peter Scoulding
Picture researcher: Diana Morris

Photo acknowledgements:
All illustrations and photos © S. Chapman except: aodaodaod/Shutterstock: 4. Suwida Boonyatistarn/Shutterstock: 36cl. CRS Photo/Shutterstock: 16cl. Dchauy/Shutterstock: 5t, 17t, 32cl, 33bl. Steve Estvanik/Shutterstock: 10c. Peter Hermes Furian/Shutterstock: 3t. Glass and Nature/Shutterstock: 5br. Halfpoint/Shutterstock: 3b. image bird/Shutterstock: 1tr, 40c. Manish Jaisi/Shutterstock: 1bg, 2-3bg, 4-5bg, 46-47bg, 48bg. Prabhjit S Kalsi/Shutterstock: 8c. 35tl. Rusian Kainitsky/Shutterstock: 37br. Kshitij30/Shutterstock: 26b. Alexandra Lande/Shutterstock: 2b. Rafael Dias Katayama/Shutterstock: 34cl. Larsek/Shutterstock: 38c. t-lorien/istockphoto: 6t. Jacqui Martin/Shutterstock: all palm fronds. Dipesh Mehrotra/Punjabi/Alamy: 9bl. reddees/Shutterstock: 35cr. Jeremy Richards/Shutterstock: 6b. Hira 41br. Phuong D. Nguyen/Shutterstock: 1br, 7t. Ninja Artist/Shutterstock: 37t. Raju Soni/Shutterstock: 47t. tratong/Shutterstock: 1bl, 19t. Utopia_88/Shutterstock: 28cl.
Every attempt has been made to clear copyright. Should there be any inadvertent omission please apply to the publisher for rectification.

ISBN 978 1 4451 5682 8

Printed in China

Franklin Watts
An imprint of Hachette Children's Group
Part of The Watts Publishing Group
Carmelite House
50 Victoria Embankment
London EC4Y 0DZ

An Hachette UK Company
www.hachette.co.uk

www.franklinwatts.co.uk

MIX
Paper from
responsible sources
FSC® C104740
FSC
www.fsc.org